The Complete Cursive Handwriting Workbook for Kids

Interior and Cover Designer: Kristine Brogno
Editor: Lia Brown
Production Editor: Erum Khan

Author photo: Twenty Toes Photography

ISBN: Print 978-1-64152-407-0

Printed in Canada

The **COMPLETE** Cursive Handwriting **WORKBOOK** for **KIDS**

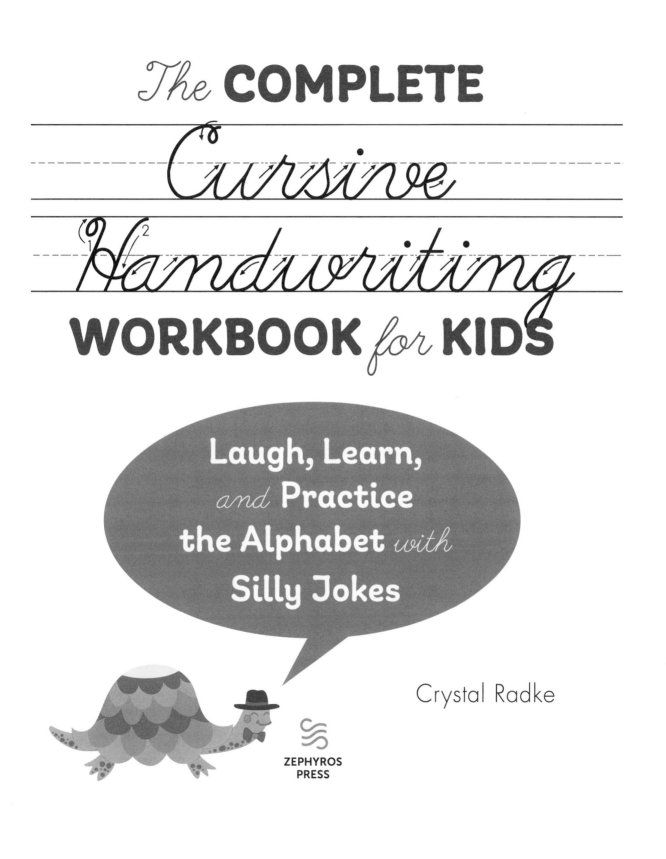

Laugh, Learn, and **Practice** the Alphabet with Silly Jokes

Crystal Radke

ZEPHYROS PRESS

Note to Parents

Learning to write in cursive is still an important skill for children today. Research suggests that learning to write in cursive activates different parts of the brain. Cursive writing also strengthens a child's fine motor skills, as it uses different muscles than when writing in print.

Children who write down what they have learned have a greater chance of retaining the information and gaining a better understanding of what they have learned. To help your child be successful, we have formatted this book in sections. First, they will learn each letter starting with capital letters and then lowercase letters. Then, they will learn to combine those letters and write words. Lastly, they will have fun using their new skills by writing jokes.

We hope you find this book helpful in teaching your child to write in cursive and that your child enjoys working through the pages of this book!

Trace and *Write* Letters

▲▽▲▽▲▽▲▽▲▽▲▽▲▽▲▽▲▽▲▽▲▽▲▽▲▽▲▽▲▽

DIRECTIONS

This section will teach you everything you'll need to learn to write each letter of the alphabet in cursive. Each page will teach you a new letter. We will start with capital letters and then learn to write lowercase letters.

For the best results, complete this workbook in order. Take your time and complete every page. Sit in your chair with your feet flat on the ground and under the table. Practice using proper pencil grasp.

Pay attention to the numbers and arrows drawn on each letter. These will show you exactly how you should form the letter and the order of your pencil strokes.

First, trace the dotted letters. Then, practice writing your letters on your own. You are on your way to writing in cursive!

Happy writing!

Apple starts with A.

Bee starts with B.

Cupcake starts with C.

Drum starts with D.

Elephant starts with E.

Fly starts with F.

Girl starts with G.

House starts with H.

Igloo starts with I.

Kite starts with K.

Juice starts with J.

Mittens starts with M.

Lion starts with L.

Nickel starts with N.

Ostrich starts with O.

Pig starts with P.

Quarter starts with Q.

Rainbow starts with R.

Snail starts with S.

Turtle starts with T.

Umbrella starts with U.

Violin starts with V.

Worm starts with W.

X-ray starts with X.

Yarn starts with Y.

Zebra starts with Z.

Trace and Write Words

DIRECTIONS

Way to go! You have learned to write the alphabet in cursive. Now, let's practice combining letters to create words. On each page, you will learn to write four different words that start with each letter in the alphabet.

To begin, trace each word and then write it on your own. Use the space provided to write each word as many times as you can. If you feel confident, try writing with a pen.

Pay attention to the first word on every line. It will include numbers and arrows to help you remember how to write each letter. You are doing great!

Happy writing!

Aa Aa Aa

am am am

ant ant ant

about about about

again again again

Bb Bb Bb

bat bat bat

boy boy boy

best best best

because because because

Cc Cc Cc

can   can   can

city   city   city

cactus   cactus

could   could   could

Dd *Dd* *Dd*

dog *dog* *dog*

drink *drink* *drink*

don't *don't* *don't*

down *down*

Ee Ee E

eave eat eat

every every every

Earth Earth Earth

elephant elephant

Ff *Ff* *Ff*

fly *fly* *fly*

fish *fish* *fish*

fire *fire* *fire*

football *football*

Gg *Gg* *Gg*

got *got* *got*

girl *girl* *girl*

given *given*

giraffe *giraffe*

Hh Hh Hh

had had had

hour hour hour

heard heard heard

horseshoe horseshoe

Ii Ii Ii

If If If

into into into

idea idea idea

igloo igloo igloo

Jj *Jj* *Jj*

jar *jar* *jar*

joke *joke* *joke*

jump *jump* *jump*

just *just* *just*

_Kk Kk Ke_

key key key

know know

kite kite kite

kitten kitten

Ll *Ll Ll*

like like like

leaf leaf leaf

little little little

blossom blossom blossom

Mm Mm Mm

map map map

mine mine mine

monkey monkey

mother mother

$\mathcal{Nm}$ $\mathcal{Nm}$ $\mathcal{Nm}$

not not not

nose nose nose

nickel nickel nickel

necklace necklace

Oo Oo Oo

on on on

$oval$ $oval$ $oval$

$orange$ $orang$

$octopus$ $octopus$

Pp Pp Pp

pig pig pig

panda panda

pizza pizza pizza

pretty pretty pretty

Qq   *Qq*   *Qq*

quist   *quist*   *quist*

quen   *quen*   *quen*

quilt   *quilt*   *quilt*

quarter   *quarter*

Rr *Rr* *Rr*

ring *ring* *ring*

nest *nest* *nest*

rocket *rocket* *rocket*

rainbow *rainbow* *rainbow*

Ss Ss Ss

She she she

sing sing sing

snake snake snake

sister sister

Tt   Tt   Tt

the   the   the

tree   tree   tree

turtle   turth

telephone   telphone

Uu Uu Uu

up up up

under under under

umbrella umbrella

unicorn unicorn

Vv Vv Vv

vest   vest   vest

violin   violin   violin

victory   victory

vegetable   vegetable

Uw Uw Uw

wet wet wet

warm warm warm

wagon wagon wagon

weather weather

Xx Xx Xx

box box box

fox fox fox

x-ray x-ray x-ray

xylophone xylophone

Yy Yy Yy Yy

yak yak yak

yo-yo yo-yo yo-yo yo-yo

yarn yarn yarn

yesterday yesterday yesterday

Zz   Zz   Z

zoo   zoo   zoo

zebra   zebra   zebra

zigzag   zigzag   zigzag

zucchini   zucchini

Trace and *Write* Jokes

▲▽▲▽▲▽▲▽▲▽▲▽▲▽▲▽▲▽▲▽▲▽▲▽▲▽▲▽▲▽▲▽▲▽▲

DIRECTIONS

Great job on writing so many words! You should be proud of yourself! Let's keeping going and have a little more fun.

Do you like telling jokes? I do! In this section of the book, you will practice tracing and writing jokes. For the first half of this section, read the joke question and trace the answer. Then, for the second half of this section, read the joke question and answer, and then write the joke in your best cursive handwriting.

Get ready to laugh, and make sure you share these jokes later with your friends. Enjoy this hilarious handwriting activity!

Happy writing
(and laughing)!

Why did the apple cry?

▲▼▲▼▲▼▲▼▲▼▲▼▲▼▲▼▲▼▲▼

Its peelings were hurt!

What do you call a bee who is having a bad hair day?

▲▽▲▽▲▽▲▽▲▽▲▽▲▽▽

A frisbee!

Why did the mouse stay inside?

▲▽▲▽▲▽▲▽▲▽▲▽▲▽▲▽▲▽▲▽

Because it was raining cats and dogs!

What did the cupcake say to the fork?

Do you want a piece of me?

What do baseball players put their food on?

▲▼▲▼▲▼▲▼▲▼▲▼▲▼▲▼

Home plates!

What did the
nose say to
the finger?

▲▽▲▽▲▽▲▽▲▽▲▽▲▽

Quit picking
on me!

What happens when two snails get in a fight?

They slug it out!

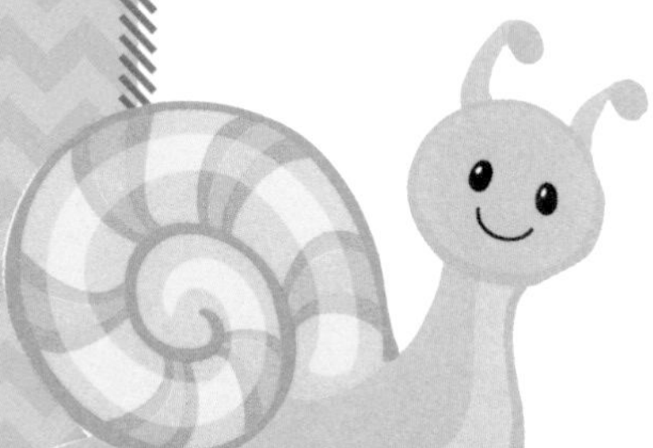

What part of a computer does a spider use?

▲▽▲▽▲▽▲▽▲▽▲▽▲▽▲▽▲▽

The web cam!

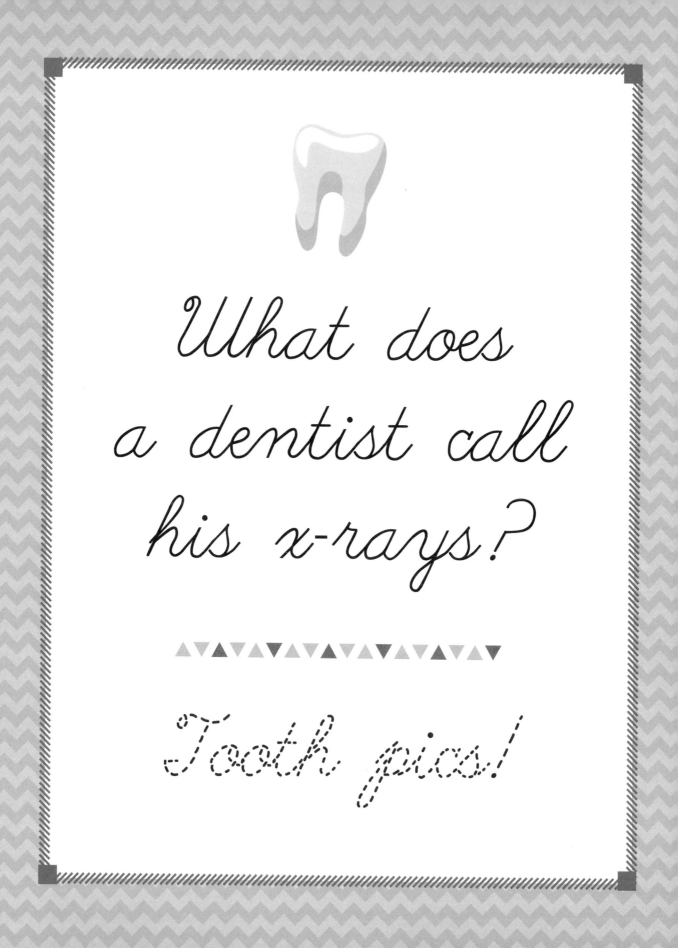

What does
a dentist call
his x-rays?

Tooth pics!

What do sheep
want to do?

Wool the
world!

What dog keeps the best time?

A watch dog!

Write the joke in cursive. Try your best!

What do fish use for money?
Sand dollars!

Write the joke in cursive. Try your best!

What does a Panda ghost eat?
Bam-boo!

Write the joke in cursive. Try your best!

What do you call a lazy baby kangaroo?

A pouch potato!

Write the joke in cursive. Try your best!

What do octopus knights wear?

A coat of arms!

Write the joke in cursive. Try your best!

What do pigs get when they're ill?
Oinkment!

Write the joke in cursive. Try your best!

Which animal is best at baseball?
A bat!

Write the joke in cursive. Try your best!

What do you call a horse that lives next door?

A neigh-bor!

Write the joke in cursive. Try your best!

_____
- -
_____
- -
_____
- -
_____
- -
_____
- -

What did the football say to the punter?
I get a kick out of you!

Write the joke in cursive. Try your best!

How do you fix a broken pizza?
With tomato paste!

Write the joke in cursive. Try your best!

_____

- -

_____

- -

_____

- -

_____

- -

_____

What is the tallest ant in the world?
A gi-ant!

Write the joke in cursive. Try your best!

This certificate is presented to

Emily Kasmierzak

for learning to write in cursive!

Date _____

About the Author

Crystal Radke is an educational leader, speaker, and writer. After spending time as a classroom teacher, she began her consultant business, where she mentors educators by providing inspirational keynotes and powerful professional development. Her degrees in Education and experience as a foster and adoptive mother have made helping children learn and grow a personal mission.